Connecting New Members
TO THE BODY OF CHRIST

by
Dr. Clarence V. Sanders

A New Member's Orientation Study Manual

SANDER'S MINISTRIES

Copyright © 2015 Dr. Clarence V. Sanders. All rights reserved.

ISBN: 978-0-578-16423-6

Sander's Ministries

Printed in the United States of America

Author Assistance Services: Mical Publishing

The work expressed in this book are solely those of the author, Mical Publishing hereby disclaims any responsibility for them.

Back cover stock images, used under license from © Shutterstock.com
VladisChern/Shutterstock.com
i3alda/Shutterstock.com

Front cover Bible Charts, Author Donnie Barnes
Barnes Bible Charts
www.biblecharts.org/thebible/thesixtysixbooksofthebible.pdf

Web addresses or links contained in this book may have changed since publication and may no longer be valid.

Unless otherwise noted, scripture quotations are taken from the King James Version of the Bible.

All rights reserved. No part of this book may be reproduced in any form, stored in a retrieval system, or transmitted by any means, by any electronic, mechanical, photocopy, or otherwise—without prior written permission of the author.

CONTENTS

About This Book vii

Dedication ix

Introduction 1

His Grace 3

New Member Orientation Study Guide 5

    Doctrinal Beliefs 5

    The Holy Scripture 5

    The Godhead 5

The Person and Work of Jesus Christ 6

    The Holy Spirit 7

    The Personality of Satan 7

    Salvation 7

The Rapture and the Second Coming 7

    Eternal State 8

 Responsibility of Believers 8

What It Means To Be A Baptist 8

 Evangelical 8

 Priesthood of the Believer 9

 Accountability 9

 Autonomy 9

Summary of Basic Beliefs 9

 The Scriptures 9

 God 9

 God the Father 10

All Believers Should Know the Basic Facts About The Church 10

Salvation 11

The Conversion Experience 13

All Believers Must Be Born Again 14

Ordinances 15

 Baptism 15

 The Lord's Supper 16

Tithes and Offerings 19

Prayer 20

Facts for Christians 21

    God the Father 21

    God the Son 23

    The Holy Spirit 24

    The Holy Bible 27

The Books of the Bible 29

The Bible 30

What Did You Learn? 31

    Review of Jesus 31

    Review of Tithes and Offerings 31

    Review of Prayer 32

    Review of the Holy Bible 32

    Review of the Holy Spirit 33

    Review of God the Father 34

    Review of the Church 35

    Review of Church Ordinances 35

    Review of the Church Body 36

Definitions 37

Order Form 39

ABOUT THIS BOOK

During my Christian walk over many years as a pastor, I have encountered many areas in which I have had to address during new members orientation, such as salvation, assurance of salvation, and resolving conflicts concerning doctrine. Also, I have found that a great number of Christians are slaves to a deep rooted habit of doubting. Not doubts as to the existence of God or the truth of the bible, but doubts are to their own personal relationship with the God in whom they profess to believe in, doubts as to forgiveness of their sins, doubts as to their hopes of heaven, and doubts based on their own inward experiences. In fact most Christians have settled down concerning their doubts. This is too often true even of believers who are struggling earnestly to live the life and walk in faith.

The intent of this book is to aid new believers in the faith and to assist all other believers in strengthening their faith and pastors or teachers to aid them in their walk with Christ in greater assurance in order to move past their doubts through addressing areas in their lives which causes the doubt. The victory has already been won and completed at the cross. The enemy has come in like a flood, but the "spirit of the Lord has lifted up a standard against him," and all doubts have been put to flight.

DEDICATION

To Him who is able to do exceedingly, abundantly above all that we ask for or think, according to the power that works in us, to him be the glory (Ephesians 3:20-21).

Welcome to New Members Orientation for Baptist Faith

By Dr. Clarence V. Sanders

INTRODUCTION

One of the most difficult yet necessary task of a growing church is the assimilation of new members into the body. Now much has been said about establishing relationships and small groups, however, in my opinion the key to developing well-grounded members is a comprehensive NEW MEMBER ORIENTATION program.

When a new convert or new member enters the fold, he or she comes with some previous indoctrination. Therefore, it is important that they are taught the basic fundamentals of the faith as quickly as possible so that they have the tools to resist the devil's attempts to derail them in their infancy. In addition, a NMO helps ease the culture shock of adapting to the new life both in and outside the church. Understanding church language such as "ordinance of the church" can become confusing without proper instruction.

The bible tells us that grace is not given through outward symbols and no ritual is "necessary for salvation." Grace is free. "But when the kindness and the love of God our Savior toward man appeared, not by works of righteousness which we have done, but according to his mercy he saved us, through the washing of regeneration and renewing of the Holy Spirit, whom he poured out on us abundantly through Jesus Christ our Savior, that having been justified by his grace we should become heirs according to the hope of eternal life" (Titus 3:4-7 NKJV). Protestants and Evangelicals see ordinances as symbolic reenactments of the gospel message that Christ lived, died, was raised from the dead, ascended to heaven, and will someday return. Rather than requirements for salvation, ordinances are visual aids to help us better understand and appreciate what Jesus Christ accomplished for us in his redemptive work. Ordinances are determined by three factors: They were instituted by Christ, taught by the apostles, and they were practiced by the early church. Since baptism and communion are the only ones which qualify under these three factors, there can be only two ordinances. This is just one example of how a new convert can be influenced by erroneous teachings. The two ordinances are to be done as the bible teaches us to follow Christ's example and not to be done to obtain salvation. Salvation can only be obtained by accepting Christ as your Savior, and not through any rites or rituals.

This tool is designed to help new members and new converts by, (1) strengthening the new convert's faith by establishing the biblical basis for what they believe, (2) dispelling any false indoctrination that will hinder them as they grow and, (3) motivating them to become an active member of the church.

That is why this book is a must have tool for pastors and teachers for New Members Orientation or assimilation.

His Transforming Grace

Church fellowship is fellowship within a church where no one has to stand alone, and provides an experience with God's people "continually devoting themselves to fellowship" (Acts 2:42B)

A church that celebrates God's glory and provides an experience with others. "The breaking of bread and prayer (Acts 2:42C).

A church that teaches the knowledge and application of God's word, and it gives us an experience with God's perspective "Continually devoting themselves to the apostles teaching." (Acts 2:42A)

A church that spreads the good news of Jesus Christ in word and in deeds, reaching others for Christ, "Go therefore and make disciples of all the nations, baptizing them in the name of the father, the son, and the Holy Spirit." Teaching them to observe all that I commanded you; and though, I am with you always, even to the end of the age. (Matthew 28:19-20)

NEW MEMBERS ORIENTATION STUDY GUIDE

Doctrinal Beliefs

Church membership is open to all who profess faith alone in Jesus Christ and are in agreement with the church's doctrinal beliefs. Please take a moment and review some beliefs, which are derived from Holy Scriptures.

The Holy Scriptures

We believe the Holy Scriptures to be the verbal, inspired words of God, authoritative, and without error in the original manuscripts. We further believe that the scriptures of both the new and old testament are designed for our practical instructions in faith and conduct.
(2 Timothy 3:16-17; 2 Peter 1:21)

The Godhead

We believe that the Godhead eternally exists in three persons. The Father, the Son, and the Holy Spirit, and that these three are one God.
(Matthew 28:19)

The Person and Work Of The Lord Jesus Christ

We believe that the Lord Jesus Christ, the eternal son of God, came into the world that He might manifest God to men, fulfill prophecy, and become the redeemer of a lost world. To those ends, He was born of the Virgin Mary, received a human body, and a sinless human nature without ceasing to be God.
(Luke 1: 30-35; John 1:1, 14, 18; Hebrews 4:15; Philippians 2:5-11)

We believe that, in infinite love for the lost, He voluntarily accepts His Father's will and became the divinely provided sacrificial Lamb and took away the sins of the world.
(Romans 3:25-31, 2 Corinthians 5:14, Hebrews 10:5-14)

We believe that he rose from the dead in the same body, though glorified, in which he had lived and died and that he resurrected the body in the pattern of the body which ultimately will be given to all believers. *(John 20:20, Philippians 3:20-21)*

We believe that upon departing earth, He was accepted by His father and that his acceptance is a final assurance to us that His redeeming work was perfectly accomplished. *(Hebrews 1:3)*

We believe that he became head over all things to the church, which is His body, and in this ministry. He does not cease to intercede and to be an advocate for the saved.
(Luke 1:35, I Corinthians 15:1-3, Ephesians 1:22-23, Philippians 2:6-8)
(1Timothy 2:5, 1 John 2:1-2)

The Holy Spirit

We believe that the Holy Spirit, the Third Person of the trinity, dwells in every believer immediately after he places his faith in the Lord Jesus Christ and that God provides, through the Holy Spirit, power to live the Christian life. *(Romans 5:5; 8:1-9, Galatians 5:16-25)*

We believe that every believer receives grace from God in the form of a spiritual gift, which enables him to function as a member of the body of Christ. *(Romans 12:6, 1 Corinthians 12:7-8, Ephesians 4:11-13)*

The Personality of Satan

We believe that Satan, the devil, is the prince of demons and the declared adversary of God and man. However, when the Lord Jesus Christ died on the cross, He limited the power of the devil and guaranteed the ultimate triumph for God.
(Ephesians 2:2; I Peter 5:8; Revelations 20:10, Colossians 2:13-15)

Salvation

We believe that no one can enter the kingdom of God unless he is born again spiritually, and that the new birth of the believer comes only through faith in the Lord Jesus Christ, the son of God. We believe, also, that our redemption has been accomplished by the grace of God, and unmerited gift, witness to the unsaved world. Our common spiritual goal is to grow toward God's likeness.
(Matthew 28:18-20, Acts 2:42-47, Romans 12:5, Ephesians 4:13-16)

The Rapture and the Second Coming of Christ

We believe that a future period of great tribulations on the earth will be climaxed by the return of the Lord Jesus Christ to the earth as He went in person in the clouds with power and great glory to establish

His millennial Kingdom. But prior to this tribulation, we believe there will be the coming of the Lord Jesus Christ in the air to receive Himself into heaven both his own who are alive and remain until His coming and also who have died in Jesus Christ.
(1 Thessalonians 4:13-17; Zechariah 14:4-11, Revelations 3:10)

Eternal State

We believe that at death the spirits and the souls of those who have trusted in the Lord Jesus Christ for salvation pass immediately into his presence and then remain in conscious bliss until the resurrection of the glorified body when Christ comes for His own, where upon soul and body reunited shall be associated with Him forever in glory. All those who rejected Jesus Christ will eternally be separated from God to endure His eternal wrath forever.
(2 Corinthians 5:8, Revelations 20: 11-15, 21:1-27)

Responsibility of Believers

We believe that all believers should seek to walk by the spirit, separating themselves from worldly practices and witnessing by life and by the truths of the Holy Scripture.
(Romans 12:1-2, Galatians 5:16, 25) (2 Corinthians 5:9-17)

We believe that all believers will be judged at the judgment seat of Christ and their reward based on their faithful obedience to Him in this life. *(1 Corinthians 3:10-17)*

What It Means To Be a Baptist

The belief that the bible is God's true, inerrant, inspired, and revelatory word for man to follow.

Evangelical

Believers that embrace the core beliefs revealed in the scriptures regarding saving faith and sharing the gospel of Jesus Christ.

Priesthood of the Believer

Laypersons have the same right as ordained ministers to communicate with God, interpret scripture, and minister in Christ's name. This in no way contradicts the biblical role, responsibility, and authority of pastoral leadership and the layperson's response to it.

Accountability

Each person is accountable before God. Your family or church cannot save you. Individuals must decide for themselves whether or not to accept Jesus Christ as their savior and live accordingly.

Autonomy

Our church is free to determine its membership and direction under the headship of Christ. We may partner with other associations, churches, conventions and ministries as the Lord leads.

Summary of Basic Beliefs

The doctrinal statement of our faith and practice is called the Baptist Faith.

The Scriptures

The Holy Bible was written by man divinely inspired and is God's revelation of himself to man. It is a perfect treasure of divine instructions. It has God for its author, salvation for its end, and truth, without any mixture of error, for its matter.

God

This is the one and only one living and true God. The eternal God reveals Himself to us as Father, Son, and Holy Spirit, with distinct personal attributes, but without division of nature, essence or being.

God the Father

God as father reigns with providential care over his universe, His creations, and the flow of the stream of human history according to the purpose of His grace...God is Father in truth to those who become children of God through Faith in Jesus Christ.

All Believers should know the Basic facts about:

The Church

God calls believers into fellowship with fellow brothers and sisters in Christ. Believers are told to assemble together to encourage each other and worship. Jesus in His instructions to his disciples gives us the purpose of the church in what is known as the Great Commission. There He states:

"Go ye therefore, and teach all the nations, baptizing them in the name of the Father, the Son, and the Holy Ghost. Teaching them to observe all things whatsoever I have commanded you: and lo, I am with you always, even until the end of the world." Amen (Matthew 28:19-20)

The responsibility of the church is to spread and share the good news of the gospel through the world. To that extent members of the church have the privilege of serving God and their fellow man. Some basic responsibilities of church members are as follow:

Love the Church: Just as Christ loves believers, the church believers are to love one another and the church. There must be love among and between members of the church. Christ set the example in this area by giving Himself for the church. We as the church ought to give our time, talent, and resources to the church.

Worship the Lord: God desires the worship and praise of his people. The church is the meeting place where believers assemble to offer worship and praise to God as one. Worship and praise of God is both public and private. The church is the physical location where believers can offer uninterrupted worship and praise to God.

Serve the Lord: God calls all believers into service. God has placed within each believer a gift that is to be used to bring him glory. In service to the church we are to use those God-given gifts.

Keep God's Commandments: By adhering to God's commandments believers show their love for God. While no one is sinless all believers should always be striving to remain obedient to the word of God.

Support the Ministry: Believers provide the financial assistance needed to sustain the operations of the church. We must give financially as God has prospered us to. By properly giving to the church we are giving to ourselves. How? When believers give to God He blesses them in return.

SALVATION

Salvation is the transformation of a person's individual nature and relationship with God as a result of repentance and faith in the atoning death of Jesus Christ on the cross. All humanity stands in need of salvation which is only possible through faith in Jesus Christ. Believers are saved by grace through faith unto good works (Ephesians 2:8-10).

Because of Adam's fall, all humans required a plan of salvation. God's word assures all that accept Christ as Lord and savior that salvation belongs to them and that they are saved.

Scriptures Regarding Salvation

Deuteronomy 30:19-20
Matthew 1:21
Matthew 11:28-30
Matthew 18:14
Mark 16:15-16

Humans are unable to save themselves. God provided a means of salvation for the world and all credit belongs to God.

God provides the following through salvation

Access to God: Before Jesus suffered and died in our place for our sins, individuals only had access to God through the highest priest. But because Christ is salvation for believers all believers have access to God through Christ Jesus. There is no need to go through another human being to have access to God.

Adoption into God's family: Through salvation God has adopted and accepted believers as his children. Because of salvation believers are able to see God as their Father.

Forgiveness of Sin: All human beings commit sin. An offering to God must be rendered by the sinner to receive forgiveness. Jesus Christ is the offering to God for all believers. Salvation blots out the sinful deeds of believers and saves us from sin which, if not forgiven leads to eternal damnation.

Peace with God: Salvation removes the hostility that exists between humans and God and replaces hostility with peace. Without salvation there will always be turmoil between humans and God.

A New Life: Without salvation humans remain in the Adamic state, the nature of Adam. The state of nature causes humans to satisfy their flesh while neglecting their souls. Salvation begins with a spiritual rebirth that causes believers to live spiritually as opposed to carnally.

Deliverance from the Power of sin: Sin does not hold on to believers because God has granted believers salvation. Without salvation humans are slaves to sin. Once salvation is received, the believer is no longer a prisoner to sin.

THE CONVERSION EXPERIENCE

In order to be saved or receive salvation, a conversion, or turn must take place. In order for the conversion to take place a person must trust in God as a child has trust in his or her parents. Humans must turn to God from sin. There are three steps in this process. While they are listed here in sequence they may also occur simultaneously.

Conviction is the state humans find themselves in when they acknowledge their sinful condition. It is a remorseful condition. Once this condition is acknowledged the person must then confess of their sins.

Repentance is the second step in the conversion process. Repentance is an essential element in the salvation experience. At this point a person not only acknowledges his or her sinful state, but also realizes that turning to God is the only way out of that sinful state. When a person repents it causes heaven to rejoice. Jesus instructs his disciples to preach repentance.

Faith is the final step in the conversion process. Faith is simply trust in God for, and in all things. A person must trust that Jesus can save him or her. A person must trust that God can and will supply all of their needs. The only means of pleasing God is by trusting Him.

All Believers Must Be Born Again

Jesus tells us that the only way that an individual will see the Kingdom of God is to be born again. The rebirth is spiritual and must take place in order to be reborn. Following is a list of scriptures regarding rebirth and why it is needed.

The wages of sin is death; but the gift of God is eternal life through Jesus Christ our Lord. (Romans 6:23).

If a person is not born again, sin will lead to his or her death. Death is separation from God forever.

That if thou shalt confess with thy mouth the Lord Jesus, and shalt believe in thine heart that God hath raised him from the dead, thou shall be saved (Romans 10:9).

Rebirth involves publicly confessing Jesus Christ as Lord and belief in God and his ability to save us.

But after that the kindness and love of God our Savior toward men appeared, Not by works of righteousness, which we have done, but according to his mercy He saved us, by the washing of regeneration, and renewing of the Holy Ghost. (Titus 3:4-5)

A human's work cannot save them, Only God upholds that power.

For whosoever shall call upon the name of the Lord, shall be saved. (Romans 10:13). God promised to save all that call upon Him.

Ordinances
Ordinance is an authoritative decree or law

Jesus commands the Christian Church to observe (2) two ordinances, Baptism and the Lord's Supper. There are some basic facts that all Christians must know regarding each of these ordinances:

Baptism

The ordinance of baptism is a symbol of the believer's identification with Christ in His death, burial and resurrection (Romans 6:3, Colossians 2:12). Baptism means to be entirely immersed or submerged in water (Mark 1:5, John 3:33).

Christians must know that Baptism

was commanded by Christ (Mathew 28:19). Jesus tells believers that they must be baptized in the name of the Father, the Son and Holy Spirit.

does not save (Mark16:16). Belief in Christ saves, not baptism; it is the outward expression of believers of their willingness to follow Christ.

water is used to perform Baptism. (Acts 10:47-48, 1Peter 3:21) Water is a cleansing agent and is used symbolically for the washing away of sins.

Christians must also be baptized in Christ

Baptism into Christ signifies that believers have been buried and raised with Christ (Romans 6:3-7).

Believers are baptized by one spirit into one body. The body of Christ (1 Corinthians 12:13)

Believers are baptized into Christ. (Galatians 3:27).

Believers are buried with Christ in baptism and raised with him through faith (Colossians 2:12).

There are two types of Baptisms

Spirit Baptism
Baptism of the Spirit is the act of the Holy Spirit; when he makes us part of the body of Christ (1Corinthians 12:13). Every believer experiences this baptism. It takes place the very moment you began to believe and receive Jesus Christ as Savior (Ephesians 4:5, Colossians 2:12, 1Peter 3:21, Mark 1:4-8)

Water Baptism
By being submerged in water believers symbolize we are baptized into death, burial and resurrection of Christ. Believers are cut off from the Adamic life because of baptism into the death of Christ (Romans 6:3-7).
In order that humans be baptized they must first believe that Jesus is the Son of God. (Acts 8:37-39)

Believers must know these basic facts About the Lord's Supper

The Lord's Supper took place before the death of Christ. Jesus and his disciples went into a closed room where he washed their feet and shared with them bread and wine, which symbolizes the body and blood of Jesus Christ. As believers partake of the Lord's Supper, we must remember Christ, receive strength from Him and rededicate ourselves to him and His cause. (1 Corinthians 11:23-34)

The Lord's Supper is an established ordinance (Matthew 26:26-29, Mark 14:22-25, Luke 22:15-20, 1Corinthians 11:23-26) Jesus established the Lord's Supper and expects all believers to continue to participate in it.

The Lord's Supper was given to the church. (Luke 22:17-20), (1 Corinthians 11:18). The churches and believers are expected to remain obedient to Christ in all things.
(The Lord's Supper is memorial to the death of our Lord and Savior. (Mark 14:22)

The Lord's Supper is called:

- Communion (1Corinthians 10:16)
- The Breaking of bread(Acts 2:42,46,20:7)
- The Cup of Blessing (1 Corinthians 10:16)
- The Lord's Supper (1 Corinthians 11:20)
- The Lord's Table (1 Corinthians 10:21)

Symbols used in the Lord's Supper and their significance

- The **Table** is the place of love, fellowship, sharing and communion. It is the family table — a love feast — a meal (Leviticus 24:5-9, Psalms 23:5).
- The **Bread** (Isaiah 53:5) represents His broken body (Mathew 26:26). It is the type of Lamb that was slain.
- The **Wine** is a symbol of the Blood of Christ that was shed for our sins, which we as believers do in remembrance of the Lord. During the Lord's Supper, we ask for forgiveness of all our sins. It represents the New Covenant (Matthew 26:27).

The Believers should do as follows as they prepare to partake of the Lord's Supper

Come

- in remembrance of Christ's death on the cross for "me" (1 Corinthians 11:23-26)
- to the table with a desire to participate (Luke 22:14-15)
- in Faith (Hebrews 4:2, 11:6, Romans 14:23)
- in remembrance of what Christ did for you (1Corinthians 11: 23-26). The Israelites remembered sin. His church remembers Him.
- with thanksgiving (Luke 22:17)
- examining their hearts (1 Corinthians 11:28) making sure we are in the right standing with God and our brothers and sisters (1Corinthians 11:27, Psalms 24:3-5)
- with a repentant and thankful heart (1Corinthians 10:21)
- in a spirit of fellowship and love (1 Corinthians 10:16-17)
- in Holy Fear (Matthew 26:24, 1Corinthians 11:27-32)
- In self-examination (1Corinthians 11:28)
- With a threefold look at Christ
- A backwards look to Calvary- Jesus's death- His suffering for us.
- An upward look to Heaven- Jesus' resurrection- His ascension- sitting at the right hand of the Father.
- A forward look to Jesus' coming when we will meet Him.

Tithes and Offerings

God has a financial plan for his church. He works by plans and has a plan for everything. He had a plan when he created the earth and humans. He had a plan for the relationship between humans and himself. He has a plan for the family. He has a plan of salvation and the work of the Church. He has a plan for the financing of the work He has ordered the church to perform.

- Tithe— tenth part, especially as offered to God
- Abraham presented the tithe to the priest-king of Jerusalem, Melchizedek *(Genesis 14:18-20)*
- Jacob pledged to offer to God, a tenth of all that God would bless Jacob with *(Genesis 28:22)*

Old Testament
The Purpose of Tithing

The tithe was used for support of the Levites and the priests (Numbers 18:20-32).

The agriculture produce tithe was used for a family feast at the sanctuary celebrating God's provision. *(Deuteronomy 14:22-27)*

The third year's tithe was to be used for the care of the Levites, orphans, widows and foreigners. *(Deuteronomy 14:28-29)*.

Consequences of Disobedience Regarding Tithing

Those that were disobedient in regards to tithing were condemned with a curse from God.

Results of Tithing

Those that are obedient in tithing are blessed by God in return.

PRAYER

Prayer is the means of communication between God and believers. It is the believer's greatest weapon. It is used to both talk to and hear from God. When properly used it allows the believer to speak intimately with God and strengthen the relationship between believers and God.

Prayer is

Commanded by God

Believers must be obedient to God in all things that He has commanded them to do. Believers must always pray and never lose hope.

The means by which believers do great things

Prayer turns the request of believers into reality. Through prayer the believer can make a difference in his or her life and the lives of others that he or she shall pray for.

Taught by Christ

Believers must pray in a manner that is consistent with what Christ teaches us and it may be done daily.

Must be done in the name of Jesus
Believers must take all requests to the Father in the name of Jesus.

Is sometimes public
Jesus tells believers to go into their closets to pray both privately and publicly. (Mathew 6:6)

How should believers begin praying?

Prayer must begin with respect and admiration to God. Address God as "Our Father" (Matthew 6:9) Some other titles are: Dear Heavenly Father, Gracious Father in heaven, Our Loving Father, Dear God, to name a few.

How should Believers end prayer?

Prayer to God should always come to a close "In the name of Jesus" Believers must make request in Jesus' name because God has given Christ authority.

"Amen," should end every prayer of believers. Amen is a transliteration of Hebrew word signifying something as certain, sure and valid, truthful and faithful. It is sometimes translated, "so be it".

Facts for Christians

Genesis 1:26, 11:7, Isaiah 48:16, Luke 1:35

The God that we serve exists in three persons: (1) God the Father, (2) God the Son, (3) God the Holy Spirit. These three as one make up the Holy Trinity. All Christians must know these basics facts regarding each of them.

God the Father

God is the creator of all things. In six days God created the heaven and the earth. He created all living creatures and provided all that every creature would need to survive.

All Christians must believe that God is real. God is not the result of a vivid imagination. He is real and without faith in him we are nothing, it is God who sustains us in all things at all times.

God is a personal being. God is not an inanimate object. He is not an, it, but rather a personal being. When we search for him with our whole heart we will find him. We acknowledge His person with such titles as Father, Shepherd, Friend and Counselor to name a few.

God is a spiritual being. God is not a human being. He is a spirit. And if we are to have true communication with him it must be spiritual. Humans too are spiritual beings. The flesh is only used to house our spirits for existence here on earth. Acceptance of this fact allows believers to both hear from and speak to God.

Jehovah is the only God. The God that we serve, Jehovah, is the only true and living God. There is no other God, end of story. Some serve and worship the earth, moon, or sun. Others worship objects made by man. Christians serve the God that created the earth, moon, and sun. We worship the God that created man that made those objects.

God Hates sin. God hates sin because of its end result to us, destruction and death. But because of his love for us God provided a way of deliverance from sin for us, Jesus.

God loves humans. While God does indeed hate sin he loves humans that committed sin. He loves us so much that he sent His only Son, Jesus, to suffer and die for our sins thereby granting us eternal life.

God is omniscient. Nothing is hidden from God. He has infinite knowledge, awareness and wisdom. He knows the inner most thoughts of humans. God is able to search our hearts and minds and he even knows the number of hairs on our head.

God is omnipresent. God is everywhere at all times. There are no hiding places from God. There is no place where anyone can escape the presence of God.

God is omnipotent. There is nothing or nobody in this world that is as powerful as God. He is the Almighty.

God the Son

Jesus was there in the beginning. Jesus has always existed. Jesus was present with God before the beginning. He worked with God to create everything that was created.

Jesus was foretold of in the Old Testament Scripture. God in his infinite wisdom knew that His people needed a savior. Sin held his people captive and he had to provide a way for us to escape from sin and a bridge to himself. The foretelling of the coming messiah provided hope and encouragement for his people.

Jesus was sent by God. God, because of his love for human beings, sent his son to serve as the ultimate sacrifice to cleanse our sins. God sent his very best to suffer and die in our place so that all who believe in Jesus and accept him as Lord and Savior would receive eternal life through the blood of Jesus at the cross.

Jesus was born of a woman. Jesus entered into this earth, in his human form, just as every man has since Eve gave birth to Cain; He was born of a woman. Mary gave birth to Jesus in a barn and used the manger for his bed.

Jesus died. He did not faint. He died. He did not lapse into a coma. He died. There is no refuting that fact. Everyone, on the day of his death, both enemies and loved ones all agreed that Jesus died for us.

Jesus was buried. After Jesus died his body was taken by Joseph of Arimathea and placed in a tomb that Joseph had purchased for himself. A stone was placed across the opening of the tomb and Pilate sent soldiers to guard the tomb.

Jesus was resurrected. Neither death nor the grave had the power to hold Jesus captive. Jesus overcame them both for our sake.

Jesus ascended to Heaven. Jesus returned to his Father and now after having saved us intercedes on our behalf to God where he sits at the right hand in heaven today.

The Holy Spirit

The Holy Spirit was there in the beginning. The Holy Spirit was present there with God, The Father, and The Son before the beginning.

The Holy Spirit is personal, not impersonal. The spirit is revealed as Him, not as an "it." The Holy Spirit is the direct agent between heaven and earth in this gospel age.

The Holy Spirit regenerates. The Holy Spirit converts or reforms us, believers, completely.

The Holy Spirit teaches. When we study the word of God, we must ask for the aid of the Holy Spirit to teach us the information that God desires us to have knowledge of.

The Holy Spirit guides. In order to live a successful Christian life all Christians must rely on the guidance of the Holy Spirit. He leads believers in all truths. He will never lead us in the wrong direction or in any way that is contrary to God.

The Holy Spirit convicts believers of sins. The Holy Spirit is here to show all the truth about sin; that it is a destructive force, contrary to God and his will and that it, if not forgiven, leads to spiritual death.

The Holy Spirit gives inspiration. The Holy Spirit gives insight and inspiration to all believers.

The Holy Spirit provides comfort; The Holy Spirit comforts believers in restless times. There are times in the life of a believer when the circumstances in life seem unbearable. God in His infinite wisdom has sent the Holy Spirit to comfort believers at such times.

The Holy Spirit is a gift from God. God has sent the Holy Spirit to believers as a gift. He expects His children to make use of all that he provides.

The Holy Spirit is a helper to believers. God Knows that believers cannot survive in this hostile world without someone helping them. His Holy Spirit Helps believers to navigate the sometimes harsh environments of this world.

THE HOLY BIBLE

"Bible" derives from the Greek term "book" and refers to the old and new testaments. God's Holy Scriptures, the Holy Bible, was written by men divinely inspired by God and it records God's revelation of himself to humans. It has God, the Holy Spirit for its author, salvation for its end, and truth without mixture of error for its matter. The bible above all talks about God and his relationship to the world. The Bible is a rule or standard of authority for Christians.

The bible is divided into two parts. The Old Testament which was primarily written in Hebrew, with some portions of Ezra—Nehemiah and Daniel in Aramaic, consists of 39 books. The New Testament which was written in Greek consists of 27 books. Combined, there are 66 books in the entire bible.

The Books of the Bible

THE OLD TESTAMENT
5 Books of Law
Genesis
Exodus
Leviticus
Numbers
Deuteronomy
12 Books of History
Joshua
Judges
Ruth
1st Samuel
2nd Samuel
1st King
2nd King
1st Chronicles
2nd Chronicles
Ezra
Nehemiah
Esther
5 Books of Poetry
Job
Psalms
Proverbs
Ecclesiastes
Song of Solomon
17 Books of Prophecy
Isaiah
Jeremiah
Lamentations
Ezekiel
Daniel
Hosea
Joel
Amos
Obadiah
Jonah
Micah
Nahum
Habakkuk
Zephaniah
Haggai
Zechariah
Malachi

THE NEW TESTAMENT
4 Gospels
Matthew
Mark
Luke
John
1 History
Acts
21 Letters
Romans
1st Corinthians
2nd Corinthians
Galatians
Ephesians
Philippians
Colossians
1st Thessalonians
2nd Thessalonians
1st Timothy
2nd Timothy
Titus
Philemon
Hebrews
James
1st Peter
2nd Peter
1st John
2nd John
3rd John
Jude
1 Revelation
Revelation

The Bible

- is life to believers(Deuteronomy 8:3)
- enlightens believers(Psalms 119:103-105)
- is knowledge and power to believers(Matthew 22:29)
- offers comfort to believers (Romans 15:4)
- tells believers that God loved him first (1John 4:19)
- list the Commandments of God (Matthew 36-40, Mark 12:28-31)
- informs believers of the fact that God is Shepherd to his people (Psalms 23)
- tells believers of the power of faith
- tells believers about the power of God over all things
- tells believers of the power of prayer and praise
- tells believers that we are all sinners
- tells believers that they are free from sin
- tells believers that they must act on what they hear and see from the word of God
- tells believers that their faith is displayed in their actions
- tell believers that Jesus will return

WHAT DID YOU LEARN?

Review of Jesus

1. Jesus did not die   True or False
2. Jesus never left heaven   True or False
3. Jesus died for the sins of the world   True or False
4. The Old Testament does not mention Jesus   True or False
5. Jesus is the Son of God   True or False
6. Jesus was baptized   True or False
7. Jesus never obeyed Joseph or Mary   True or False
8. Jesus is now in Heaven   True or False
9. Jesus did not resist temptation   True or False
10. Jesus was resurrected   True or False

Review of Tithes and Offerings

1. What percentage of a person's income is the tithe?
   _____

2. What is the purpose of the tithe?
   A. Numbers 18:20-23
   B. Deuteronomy 14:22-27
   C. Deuteronomy 14:28-29

3. What are the consequences disobedience brings regarding tithing? (Malachi 3:10-12)
   _____

4. What are the results of being obedient regarding tithing? (Malachi 3:10-12)
   _____

5. What did Jesus say should not be neglected even when a person tithes? (Matthew 23:23)_____

Review of Prayer

1. Believers should never pray in public

   True or False

2. Jesus did not teach on prayer

   True or False

3. Prayer is needed in critical moments

   True or False

4. Prayer was commanded by God

   True or False

5. Believers don't have to pray in the name of Jesus   True or False

6. A prayer should never end with Amen
   True or False

7. Prayer is not the way to communicate
   True or False

8. Prayer is a time to speak and not listen
   True or False

9. Prayer strengthens the relationship between God and man   True or False

Review of the Holy Bible

1. The Bible is divided into two parts, they are _____ and _____.

2. How many books make up the Old Testament? _____

3. How many books are there total in the bible? _____

4. Who is the author of the Bible?_____.

5. The Bible tells believers that their _____ is displayed in their actions? (James 2:14)

6. The bible does not tell believers that Jesus will return.
   True or False

7. The bible tells believers that there is power in their praise?
   True or False

8. The Bible tells believers that they loved God first.
   True or False

9. The bible tells believers that they can never be free from sin.
   True or False

10. God is the Shepherd of His people.
    True or False

Review of the Holy Spirit

1. The Holy Spirit provides _____ for believers.
   (John 14:16)

2. The Holy Spirit is a _____ from God.
   (John 14:16)

3. The Holy Spirit _____ believers of sin.
   (John 16:8-11)

5. When believers need help they can call on _____
   (Romans 8:26)

6. The Holy Spirit _____all believers.
   (2nd Corinthians 3:6)

7. God the father, Son and _____ were there in the beginning. (Genesis 1:26, 11:7)

Review of God the Father

1. What does God hate?
   _____

2. God is everywhere at all times. This is called?
   _____

3. God exist is three persons. Who are they?
   _____, _____, _____

4. What did God create?
   _____

5. God has all Power. What is this called?
   _____

6. How did God show his love for the world?
   _____

7. Who is God? (Numbers 23:19, John 4:24)
   _____

8. All Christians must believe that God is (Hebrews 11:6)
   _____

Review of the Church

1. Believers are not required to serve God.
   True or False

2. Jesus loved the Church.
   True or False

3. God does not desire the worship of believers.
   True or False

4. Believers should support the ministry.
   True or False

5. Believers don't have to share the gospel.
   True or false

6. Believers don't have to keep God's commandments
   True or False

7. Believers serve God and man.
   True or False

Review of Church Ordinances

1. How many ordinances are there in the church?
   _____
2. What are those ordinances?
   _____
3. Bread and wine represents the _____ of Jesus Christ.
4. What are the three words used to describe the Lord's Supper.
        A.
        B.
        C.

5. Believers that came to partake in the Lord's Supper where?

   _____

6. The table is a place of_____ and _____

7. What are the two types of baptisms?_____ and_____

8. Does baptism save sinners? _____

9. Did Jesus command believers to be baptized? _____

10. What property is used to perform baptism? _____

Review of the Church Body

1. Because of salvation believers are forgiven of sins.
      True or False

2. Because of salvation believers have peace with God.
      True or False

3. God saves all who call upon Him.
      True or False

4. What are the three steps in the conversion experience?
   _____, _____
   _____.

5. What is the change in the life of a believer?
   _____

6. The wages of sin is? _____

7. Salvation delivers believers from the_____.

8. Repentance is the_____ step in the conversion experience.

IN MY OPINION THIS IS HOW THE FOLLOWING SUBJECTS ARE DEFINED

1. CHRISTIAN OUTREACH—To reach outwardly and to extend an invitation of welcome into the worship setting that others may encounter Jesus Christ and accept him as Savior.

2. CHRISTIAN WITNESSING—Christian witnessing is sharing our heartfelt faith in Jesus Christ to others of the goodness of God, with the expectation that they may accept Christ as Savior.

3. CHRISTIAN TESTIMONY—Sharing your personal encounter with Jesus and testifying to his saving grace that they may accept Christ.

End Note

Give a man a Fish: Chinese proverb: Attribution —"The Quotation Page," Moncur's Motivational Quotations, accessed May 5, 2015, http// www.quotationspage.com/quote/2279.html.

Thank you for your participation in this New Member Orientation study guide. For other writings by Dr. Sanders such as *"Where Is Jesus when I am Hurting"* and *"Finding Peace through Prayer"* go to www.authorhouse.com

CONNECTING NEW MEMBERS TO THE BODY OF CHRIST

A New Member's Orientation Study Manual

ORDER FORM

To order your copies of this book please complete this form and mail to:

C. Sanders
P.O. Box 221
Blanchard, LA 71009
Make checks payable to: C. Sanders

Cost: $14.95 each for a single copy
For inquiries regarding multiple copies at a reduced price plus Shipping and Handling please email:
cvsanders@bellsouth.net

Name_____

Address_____

City _____ State _____ Zip Code _____

Phone_____ Date of Order_____

Signature_____

Number of books ordered _____ x $14.95 $____

Shipping and handling: $1.50 per book $____

Subtotal $____

Total $____

PAYMENT (Check One)

☐ Check

☐ Money Order

www.ingramcontent.com/pod-product-compliance
Lightning Source LLC
Chambersburg PA
CBHW071416290426
44108CB00014B/1850